Nigel Cawthorne is the author of over 150 books – everything from *Flight MH370 – The Mystery* to *Sex Lives of the Kings and Queens of England*. He was called to testify to the US Senate over *The Bamboo Cage*. *The Iron Cage* prompted questions in both houses of the British parliament. *Sex Lives of the US Presidents* got him on the *Joan Rivers Show* and *Sex Lives of the Popes* got him on the biggest chat show in Brazil. He lives in London.

GU00985751

Other books by Nigel Cawthorne

*The Empress of South America – The Irish Courtesan Who Destroyed
    Paraguay and Became Its National Heroine*
Flight MH370 – The Mystery
The Bamboo Cage – The True Story of American POWs in Vietnam
The Iron Cage – Are British POWs Still Alive in Siberia?
*Daughter of Heaven – The True Story of the Only Woman to Become
Emperor of China*
Takin' Back My Name – The Confessions of Ike Turner
Reaping the Whirlwind – Voices of the Enemy from World War II
Che Guevara – The Last Conquistador
Sex Lives of the Popes
Sex Lives of the US Presidents
Sex Lives of the Great Dictators
Sex Lives of the Kings and Queens of England
Sex Lives of the Hollywood Goddesses
Sex Lives of the Hollywood Idols
Sex Lives of the Great Artists
Sex Lives of the Great Composers
Sex Lives of the Hollywood Goddesses 2
Sex Lives of the Famous Gays
Sex Lives of the Famous Lesbians
Sex Lives of the Roman Emperors
Strange Laws of Old England
Curious Cures of Old England
Amorous Antics of Old England
Sex Secrets of Old England
Beastly Battles of Old England
Flight MH370: The Mystery
Vietnam: A War Lost and Won
House of Horrors
Jack the Ripper's Secret Confession
A Brief History of Robin Hood
A Brief Guide to James Bond
A Brief History of Sherlock Holmes
A Brief Guide to Jeeves and Wooster
A Brief Guide to JRR Tolkien
A Brief Guide to Agatha Christie – Queen of Crime
The King of Crime Writers – The Biography of John Creasey

Jeremy

Clarkson:

Motormouth

Nigel Cawthorne

First published by Endeavour Press Ltd in 2014.

© Nigel Cawthorne 2014

Copyright for the cover image belongs to Feature Flash: <a href="http://www.shutterstock.com/gallery-842245p1.html?cr=00&pl=edit-00">Featureflash</a> / <a href="http://www.shutterstock.com/?cr=00&pl=edit-00">Shutterstock.com</a>

ISBN 978-1501039324 (paperback)

ASIN: B00KYPORBO (ebook)

To my older brother Graham, who was Jeremy Clarkson to the life and down the pub.

Table of Contents

Introduction

On television, I find Jeremy Clarkson loathsome and obnoxious. But I guess he wants me to feel that way. Maybe I am just jealous, because he is very funny too. And as a writer, I admire him immensely. He is brilliant on the page. His use of metaphor, imagery, phrasing and – excuse me for being an anorak here – his inventive use of punctuation make his prose sing.

George Orwell said that good writing is like a window pane. You can see through it without anything of the author getting in the way. Clarkson's prose isn't like that. It is like sucking on a bong. Or, better, inhaling ether. It fills you with a kaleidoscope of ideas; it makes you high. (I note here that I have never found Mr Clarkson use a semi-colon or, for that matter, brackets.) Like Shakespeare (who he loathes), you know to have written as he has written he must have been drunk. On words.

Orwell also said: "One can write nothing readable unless one constantly struggles to efface one's own personality". Needless to say Jeremy doesn't do that either. What would be the point? Reading Clarkson, you get Clarkson. On speed, appropriately enough. And he uses the same Psychocoaster technique in his TV scripts.

On television, Clarkson is larger than life. He is the embodiment of a certain type of macho. Not the posturing Latin variety, but the sort you get with the lads down the pub. This does not seem to put women off. Some 40 per cent of the audience for *Top Gear* is female. And that audience is massive. Each show pulls in some 350 million viewers in 170 countries. According to the *Guinness Book of Records* it is the most widely watched factual TV show in the world and the franchise is thought to be worth $1.5 billion.

Although there are two other presenters on the show, it is Clarkson who takes the plaudits and fends off the brickbats. He is the star who has built it up from being a minor motoring programme on a minority TV channel to a global phenomenon.

His secret is simple. Both on air and in his newspaper columns, he says what he thinks – about cars and any other subject under the sun – usually in the most robust fashion imaginable. This book is about what makes him tick. It is not for the faint-hearted. Anyone who reads the *Guardian*, eats muesli or wears sandals should look away now.

Nigel Cawthorne

Bloomsbury, May 2014

Chapter One – Bear Child

Jeremy Clarkson is a bluff Yorkshireman. He says what he thinks and does not care whether you like it or not. He was born on 11 April 1960 in Doncaster, an industrial town in West Riding. His father, Edward, was a travelling salesman; his mother, Shirley, a part-time teacher, who went on to become a magistrate.

She was from Doncaster itself. Eddie came from Tickhill, a small village some five miles to the south. Until their marriage in 1957, he had been the black sheep of the family and had struggled to make his way in the world. However, he was known as a snappy dresser and, at the age of twenty-four, was nuts about cars. A month before their wedding he had wrapped his boss's car around a bus stop, breaking a number of bones and ending up in Doncaster Royal Infirmary. On their wedding day he was still wearing a cast, leading the local newspaper to carry the caption to their wedding photo: "Groom plastered before the wedding starts." Their honeymoon was a driving tour of Ireland. Returning to Yorkshire Eddie had another five motoring accidents in quick succession and meeting a brewer's lorry on a humpback bridge in thick fog put him back in hospital. Nevertheless, Shirley fell pregnant in 1959. She was offered two new anti-morning sickness drugs that had just come on the market. One was Thalidomide. She took the other one.

Born by Caesarian section, her first child was christened Jeremy Charles Robert Clarkson. Two years later she gave birth to his younger sister Joanna. With two young children the Clarksons moved out of their small cottage into a near derelict farmhouse in Burghwallis, a tiny hamlet some five miles north of Doncaster, and began to do it up. The family was by no means rich, but World War II had been over fifteen years before Jeremy was born. The years of austerity were behind them. Prime Minister Harold Macmillan had already told the British people: "You've never had it so good." Economist John Kenneth Galbraith had announced the birth of "the affluent society" and the age of consumerism, which would be Jeremy's métuer, had begun.

The Clarksons were convinced of the benefits of a good education and they were prepared to pay for it. When it was time for Jeremy to enrol in the local prep school, Shirley became a full-time teacher to help pay the fees. Otherwise the young Clarkson had little to worry about. His father was a gifted salesman. Within their stable family, there was plenty of room for teasing.

"When I was growing up, we laughed at every calamity that struck," he said. "You fall over. Laugh. Someone's nasty to you. Laugh. Life is short and you haven't time to be stuck in traffic jams or be sad."

It was a habit that Clarkson continued throughout his life. At the age of forty-five, when his father was gravely ill, he was still asking his mother: "List all the illnesses dad has had this month"; or "Name all the drugs that dad's taking beginning with the letter P."

4

"It's just what we do," Shirley said. "It's more constructive than getting depressed."

The only cloud on the horizon was Shirley's mother who suffered from mental illness and would make off in her Morris Minor. Shirley's father, a GP, would head off after her in his Bentley.

To get away from it all, the young Clarkson family went on camping holidays in France. On one of these trips in 1970, Eddie had another accident. He slipped on some rocks and damaged his arm. His temperature soared. He fell unconscious and amputation was mentioned. To prevent this, Shirley was determined to get him home. Loading him into their brand new Ford Cortina, they headed back to England and raced up the M1. In Doncaster Infirmary, Eddie pulled through. The car did not. It had a leaky oil sump and the high-speed journey had taken its toll. The big end was gone. It was cranked aboard a low-loader, never to be seen again.

Destined for public school, the young Clarkson needed extra maths lesson. They did no good. At the age of forty-eight, he still could not divide by twelve, Shirley said. Nevertheless, to make a little extra to pay for the lesson, she turned to dressmaking and making soft furnishings to sell to neighbours. Then she began selling a line of tea cosies to a kitchen shop in Doncaster.

It has to be said that Shirley came from a long line of entrepreneurs. Her great-great grandfather, John Kilner, made a fortune in the early 1800s manufacturing the Kilner jar, a screw-top glass jar with a rubber seal used for storing food. However, foreign competition led to the closing of the factory. Some of the money from the sale of the patents was said to have been used to buy a car in 1901, which would have made it one of the first cars in Yorkshire. Then a family rift led the inheritance to be passed to a distant cousin.

Soon making tea cosies was bringing in as much money as Shirley's salary as a teacher. So she gave up the classroom and began producing a line of novelty tea cosies, draft excluders and pouffes under the name Gabrielle Designs. The company did so well that Eddie gave up his job to join the business. When they told Jeremy of their decision to go into partnership, he was unimpressed. His only response was: "Okay, now can we watch *Thunderbirds?*" on their newly acquired television set.

As the business took off, they bought another Cortina, this time second-hand. It was followed by an Audi, then a BMW which were used to ferry the children around. His numerous accidents had not dampened Eddie's passion for cars. This was matched by young Jeremy who collected Dinky toys, crashing them into the skirting boards and forcing Joanna to play hot-wheels. With him as an older brother, she never stood a chance of becoming "girlie".

They had a Springer Spaniel which Jeremy called "Thingy". She gave birth to a litter of five puppies called Genesis, Exodus, Leviticus, Numbers and Deuteronomy after the first five books of the bible. One day, Numbers was found mating on the village war memorial, which was on a street so narrow that the bus could not pass until they had uncoupled. This amused the young Clarkson immensely.

For Christmas each year, Shirley made cuddly toys for the children – Winnie the Pooh, Eeyore, Tigger. In 1971, she came across the book *A Bear Called Paddington* by Michael Bond. That Christmas, she gave them a homemade Paddington Bear. When the children's friends saw it, they wanted one too. The bear was so popular that Shirley decided to market it. Michael Bond gave his imprimatur and took a royalty. But there was one problem – the Bear would not stand up. She solved this problem by putting it in toddler's Wellington boots. Sales rocketed. This is how Paddington Bear go his famous Wellingtons and how Paddington Bear paid for Jeremy Clarkson to go to public school.

Chapter Two – Gift of the Gab

The success of Gabrielle Designs and Paddington Bear meant that Jeremy's parents had little spare time to bring up him and his sister. Both were sent to public schools far away. The young Clarkson had already literally outgrown home. The family's four-hundred-year-old farmhouse had low ceilings. By the age of fourteen he was already six foot tall and was hitting his head on the beams. But the one thing that lured him home was his father's love of cooking. Sometimes Jeremy would arrive home with a bunch of school friends for an impromptu feast which Eddie was only too delighted to lay on.

While his father cooked, his mother made herself the life and soul of the party. She could hold any room spellbound with her wild anecdotes. Clarkson took after her. "I was always a bit of a mother's boy," he said.

It was his grandfather who introduced Jeremy to the high-life. He took the young Clarkson to fancy restaurants where he got a taste for langoustines and lobster thermidor.

Despite the backing of Paddington Bear, Clarkson was not destined to excel academically. As early as the age of eleven, Clarkson had lost interest in education. He went from top of the class to the bottom overnight. Maths and physics, he said, would be no good to him. He told his mother that he was going to become Alan Wicker, an astronaut or King. Shirley said she found him a handful even before he was shipped off to boarding school.

Though Jeremy Clarkson does not come across as a swanky type, he went to the upmarket public school Repton in Derbyshire. Incorporating parts of a twelfth-century priory, the school had been in existence for four hundred years. Old boys included real-life *Chariots of Fire* athlete Harold Abrahams, actor Basil Rathbone, author Roald Dahl, comedian Graeme Garden, tennis player Bunny Austin, mayor of London Carole Blackshaw, Hong Kong chief justice Andrew Li QC and a number of distinguished academics. Clarkson would not be joining their number.

Arriving at Repton was a shock. From being top of the pile at his prep school, Clarkson was now right down at the bottom. Rebellion was in order. He was determined to be Jack the Lad and turned to drinking and smoking. Although he was a constant vexation to the masters, he felt he fitted in at boarding school.

"My only disappointment was that no one ever tried to bugger me," he said. He felt that he had missed out on an important part of growing up. He also hated the school food.

A precocious lad, the pubescent Clarkson soon had an eye for the girls. Around town in the holidays, he found it vital to wear the right jeans. These were the seventies and he wore flares that had to fall exactly a quarter of an inch over the sole of his platform shoes. Then came punk. He was a fan of The Clash and his jeans then had to have holes in them.

By this time, his parents were in despair. They were frequently summoned his school to see the headmaster. Jeremy would lay in wait for them outside the school to explain that he had not done whatever he had been accused of and there had been some horrible misunderstanding. He already had the gift of the gab. His crimes included constantly needling the masters, sneaking out from games to visit the local girls' school and breaking wind during the two-minutes silence. Eventually, his headmaster could stand no more and he was asked to leave – or, in other accounts, he was expelled. This happened before he even took his A-levels. He would not be going to university. His parents considered all the money they had spent on his education wasted. His sister, by contrast, did well at school and went on to be a corporate lawyer.

But the young Clarkson was developing in other ways. At seventeen, he passed his driving test in his grandfather's R-type Bentley. Then came his first car – a Ford Cortina 1600E with a tweaked GT engine, wooden dashboard trim, Lotus designed suspension and Rostyle alloy wheels. Clarkson taped a picture of Debbie Harry to the middle of the steering wheel. It was, Clarkson said, "a cool car". Somehow he resisted a pair of furry dice.

Back at home with his parents, Jeremy remained a burden. Fortunately his grandfather knew the editor of the local paper in nearby Rotherham and Clarkson was taken on as a trainee on the *Rotherham Advertiser*. It was there that he learnt his trade. He did not enjoy small-town reporting, but stuck it out for three years and took block-release courses at a Sheffield college. Meanwhile, he upgraded to a VW Scirocco.

After losing it at a village flower show, Clarkson quit the paper. With scant qualifications, his prospects were poor. For lack of any alternative, he became a rep for the family firm. His patch covered anything south of The Wash and he was something of a success as a salesman. His mother said: "He went down a bomb with most customers, but the odd few, those without a sense of humour, did ring us to complain. His petrol expenses were ludicrously high, and he wore out tyres at a horrific rate, but he was happy, I think."

He was not particularly committed and sales came a poor second to his social life. He would plan his route so that he would end up within easy reach of a party, say, in Fulham. That meant that shops in Penzance would have to open their doors to him before 9am or never get a visit. And he refused to work on weekends.

Eventually his father put his foot down. Jeremy was despatched to meet an important overseas buyer in a hotel in London's West End where he was to sell the man their latest line – Welephant. But the buyer had never heard of the famous red elephant before. "They're everywhere," said Clarkson. Then, but a stroke of luck, a man in a Welephant suit came rushing into the hotel foyer to use the loo. "You see," said Clarkson. "Here's one now."

His other coup at Gabrielle Designs was to negotiate a deal with the explorer Sir Ranulph Fiennes. The family firm were to make a toy dog to help promote Fiennes' Transglobe Expedition. Clarkson manned a stall in the lobby of a cinema showing the film of Fiennes' trek across the Antarctic with his latest girlfriend who turned up in a see-through dress. This attracted Prince Charles who was also attending the premiere. He made off with one without paying. The contribution sales of the toy dog made to the funds of the expedition was precisely nil.

Nevertheless Jeremy's work in the continued success of Gabrielle Designs gave him enough money to leave home. He moved to Fulham where he lived with three friends in a flat they called the Vomitarium.

"It was all vomit-stained walls and curry packets – the house from hell," he says. "What little money we had went on booze and fags. Women didn't like coming around. But once they did, that was it because they stuck to the carpet and couldn't get out."

Though money was tight, Clarkson did have plenty of girlfriends and, despite his colourful recollections, he was not exactly slumming it. One of his neighbours, he later discovered, was Lady Diana Spencer.

Clarkson was not really cut out to be a salesman. He enjoyed rubbing people up the wrong way too much. But with no qualifications to speak of, he had little other choice. However, on the *Rotherham Advertiser* he had learned he could write. He also had a passion for cars and found all the motoring publications then available deadly dull. So, with fellow journalist Jonathan Gill, he started the Motoring Press Agency. Through it, he picked up a syndicated motoring column that ran in the local press. Otherwise the agency was not a success. After three years, he found himself deeply in debt. However, he was on the circuit and got invited to all the new car launches.

Perched on the edge of a financial abyss, he was forced to do what all other motoring journalists did and spend his column rehearsing statistics – fuel efficiency, acceleration, torque ratios. That was not his style at all. He was more interested in the sheer excitement of driving and what a car said about its driver. In the introduction to *Jeremy Clarkson's Hot 100: Cars that Make You Go PHWOAR!* he says: "You see, a car is rather more than the sum of its parts. To argue that a car is simply a means of conveyance is like arguing that Blenheim Palace is simply a house."

He stayed out of the anoraky world of rocker valves and idler gears. "Yeah, people are always keen to talk about that stuff, particularly the Germans. They love the details. They love to get you down and say, 'Look at our new track rod end. Have you ever seen anything like it?' And I say, sorry, I don't think it's very important. I don't think the vast majority of people who buy cars care a gnat's what is under the bonnet. Just so long as, when they pull out to overtake a tractor, they'll go faster than the tractor."

It was during this period that Clarkson had married for the first time. He met convent-educated Alexandra James when she was seventeen and he was twenty-two. At nineteen she set up her own company offering secretarial services. They shared a one-bedroom flat which, she complained, stank of cigarettes. She did not consider him much of a catch.

Then in 1988, he was at a car launch when he sat beside a man named Jon Bentley. They immediately hit it off and Clarkson made Bentley laugh with his irreverent comments about the vehicle being launched and the company who made it. But Bentley was not just another motoring hack. He was the new producer of the BBC's long-running motoring programme *Top Gear*. It had been broadcast since 1977 and Bentley was looking for a way to refresh it. He thought that employing this outspoken word-slinger might do the trick. Again Jeremy Clarkson's gift of the gab had set him in good stead.

Chapter Three – Petrosexual

It was discovered immediately that Jeremy Clarkson was a natural on TV. His long face, mass of curly hair and height – he was 6ft 5in – were distinctive and well suited to the small screen. His voice had a deep, broad Yorkshire tone. He was direct, entertaining and made people laugh. While he could talk knowledgeably about cars, he used the strategic pause and an uneven stress on certain words to convey an attitude that others eschewed. Back then, his performance was restrained, but polished.

Clarkson had only just started his television career when his first wife left him, complaining that he was a "lazy and opinionated slob" who was "too big for his boots". He always wanted to be the centre of attention and no one could get a word in edgewise. She never thought he would amount to anything and left him for one of his friends who had been a guest at their wedding.

He was distraught and, she claimed, he cut up all her clothes and lost five stone in weight. She also claimed that she was the only person who ever broke his heart and that losing her gave him extra drive and was the real force behind his career.

At the time, though, she felt sorry for him and perhaps a little guilty about leaving him, so she contrived to get him together with a mutual friend, Frances Catherine Cain, known to her friends as Francie. She was a career woman – a redundancy counsellor with her own flat and a Golf GTI, which would become one of Clarkson's "Hot 100". When they had met ten years early, she was terrified of him. He was over a foot taller than her, loud and bossy. He was a little frightened of her too. She seemed awfully grown up. Nevertheless, they grew to be friends.

After Alex had left him, he and Francie got drunk one night and he stayed over in her flat. The next day she was going on holiday to Greece. He turned up at the airport with a ticket and his bag packed. They spent the first week of her holiday together. Then he had to leave. He missed her birthday and when he met her at the airport he was loaded down with presents. Soon he moved in with her.

By then he was appearing regularly on *Top Gear*, but he was still not making much money and was mired in debt. However, things changed when a new production team took over the programme in 1992 and he was given his head. He had already developed his trademark long pause before delivering the coup de grace after forgetting his lines during his second road test.

Clarkson proposed to Francie on a trolley car in San Francisco and they married in Fulham in 1993. They were taken from the church to the reception in a Dodge Viper, another of his "Hot 100". As well as his wife, Francie became his manager.

Encouraged to be forthright by the producers, he was beginning to make his mark on the show. And he could be damning. He said that a Toyota Corolla G6 was "the most idiotic way of blowing £14,000". This was a new departure in the deferential world of motoring journalism and the company refused to let him test drive any more of its cars. Vauxhall did the same after he trashed the Vectra. "It's just a box on wheels," he said. "It's like to trying to road test a microwave oven." It was years before he was forgiven.

His rudeness made him stand out from the other presenters. As the ratings climbed, the producers egged him on. Before long, he was taking a FSO Polonez Leisure – or FSO Polonez Digusting, as he called it – hoisting it on a crane, then played conkers with another Polonez dangling from another, then dropping them on a concrete runway.

These excesses soon made him a celebrity. People recognized him in the street. The *Sunday Times* took him on as a car critic and the BBC began to exploit his talent in other ways. In 1995, they commissioned *Jeremy Clarkson's Motorworld*. This involved Clarkson travelling around the world exploring the car culture of selected nations. And it was sexy. In Italy, he said Ferrari was "a pagan god, a steel deity, sex on wheels". The Lamborghini Diablo was a "5.7-litre vibrator, a truck and a chest of drawers with rocket motor in the boot. If you want a wild ride, this is where you queue." But a man in a Ferrari 355, he said, feels "like he's just had sex with Claudia Schiffer and Elle Macpherson. At the same time." Meanwhile the Alfa V6 is "pure opera".

"While every motor in the world sounds like someone singing in the bath, this is full Pavarotti," he said. "People who would rather have their legs amputated than talk about cars will actually ask what on earth is under the bonnet – the London Symphony Orchestra or the Berlin Philharmonic? One girl asked me to stop revving the engine so high because she kept sticking to the seat."

The imagery was both rich and provocative. Pure Clarkson.

Visiting Detroit, he manages to cite *Robocop*, soul music and Gertrude Stein within a paragraph. The mayor tells him that Detroit is going to be the next great international city and a great place to do business. Clarkson says: "And I am a teapot."

Other stops on the itinerary were Japan, Vietnam, India – home of the Hindustan Ambassador "better known as the 1950s Morris Oxford" – and Iceland, which involved dare-devil off-road driving in a customized four-wheel-drive van.

Later he wrote: "Eagle-eyed viewers of the Iceland programme might have noticed that at no point did I actually appear on the glacier. This is because, at the time, I was in a hospital in Chelsea with my wife who had gone into labour two weeks early. As the crew stood up there, with blue ears, I was watching the doctors deliver Emily." Elsewhere, he says this is not true. He missed the birth of his daughter because he was filming in Iceland. Take your pick.

The following year took him to Monaco, Switzerland, Australia, Texas, Dubai and Cuba, where he gloried in the jury-rigged Chevy Impalas, Cadillac Coupe de Villas and other American cars from the 1940s and 1950s that still plied the streets of Havana. Then he did a Christmas special on the UK – home of "the best drivers in the world, by a country mile".

"You may think that making *Motorworld* was one long orgy of fast cars, loose women, supersonic boats and high living," he said. "But you'd be forgetting the expense accounts, candle-lit dinners, the sun-kissed beaches and five-star hotels."

The series was attacked for rehearsing nation stereotypes. You should never buy French or Spanish cars, he said, "because the Frogs are our oldest enemies and the Spaniards murder bulls and can't cook."

Nevertheless *Motorworld* topped BBC Two's ratings.

The series was turned into a book which was, of course, dedicated to Francie. He followed up with *Clarkson on Cars*, *Clarkson's Hot 100* and *Plant Dagenham* about cars in film, TV, music and sport. And he kept on publishing books, usually about one a year, largely anthologies of his columns from the *Sunday Times* and *Top Gear* magazine. They ended up in the bestsellers list, usually at number one.

Clarkson feigned to be a bad father, actually admitting to changing a nappy once – Francie had been delayed at her sister's and returned home to find him wearing rubber gloves and a scuba mask with a scarf doused in Chanel wrapped around his face. He also left the house before Emily woke in the morning to avoid the traffic and got home from work after she had gone to sleep. However, she was barely six months old when he bought her a baby walker – "her first set of wheels".

While car manufacturers continued to fume at Clarkson's caustic remarks, he maintained that he had no effect in the market place.

19

When a new Ford Escort came out in 1992, Clarkson trashed it on TV. It went on to become Britain's bestselling car. He had praised the Renault A610, but it "sold six," Clarkson said. Not that he held a brief for Renault. He said, memorably: "This is a Renault Espace, probably the best of the people carriers. Not that that's much to shout about. That's like saying 'Oh good, I've got syphilis, the best of the sexually transmitted diseases!'"

He then proceeded to cut the roof off one to make it a convertible, then sawed it in half. But Clarkson said it is not his job to prop up the motor trade.

"My job is to entertain people on telly," he said. "I use cars as a prop."

The Ford Scorpio was so ugly "we spent most of the time filming it from the back so as not to frighten viewers". However, Aston Martin gave him an enormous accolade when they let him drive their Vantage supercar. He was the only person outside the company allowed to do so.

Not only did Clarkson upset the motor trade, he also riled the environmentalists – an impressive double.

"We don't have a carbon footprint," he said. "That's because we drive everywhere."

He was also happy to have a go at drivers. Of Nissan drivers, he said: "They can't park, don't understand roundabouts and are not averse, once in a while, to driving the wrong way down a motorway."

Then there was: "All BMWs are driven by people who are psychologically unfit to drive anything more powerful than an electric razor." However, four BMWs make it into Clarkson's Hot 100 and Francie drove one. But BMWs were, of course, "Nazi staff cars".

The health-and-safety lobby were after him too when he suggested that the motorway speed limit should be raised to 130 mph. Speed, he was told, kills. His riposte was that, in that case, Concorde should be the most dangerous form of travel. This was before the crash in Paris in 2000 that led to the plane's premature demise. Up until that point, in over twenty-four years of service, it had not been responsible for a single death. Clarkson's serious point was that, when people drive fast, they concentrate on what they are doing.

"Speed has never killed anyone," he said. "Suddenly becoming stationary. That's what gets you."

When an MP objected, it made no difference to Clarkson. He had little respect for MPs. He had plenty of time for Concorde though. He was on the last flight when it was retired in 2003 and wrote its obituary. For him, aeroplanes and cars have a personality, unless they are made in Japan, of course.

In 1994, Clarkson's father Eddie was prescribed a course of chemotherapy. Not that anyone thought it would do much good. His mother Shirley called him the day before she thought Eddie was going to die. Clarkson jumped in the car and drove north. The following day Francie brought sister Joanna, her husband Jon and their new-born baby Benjamin north from their home in Clapham.

Two days after his father's death, Clarkson went to Sheffield to collect his death certificate. It was a cold and drizzling day, and Clarkson remarked to the registrar that he had been in no hurry to visit Sheffield again. Visibly affronted, the registrar said: "But we've got a Supertram." Clarkson responded that an electric bus, no matter how high-tech, would not make up for the loss of his father.

On screen, the BBC raised no objection to Jeremy's untoward comments with between six and seven million views tuning in – even after he had offended great swathes of the country. Clarkson said that Norfolk people were "so interbred that they don't know the difference between a Ferguson tractor and a Ford Capri". He also called Norfolk "the dullest place on earth". As a result they started a We Hate Jeremy Clarkson Club there and made an appearance at the 1995 Motor Show.

"In a way, it's a real honour," said Clarkson. "I think almost the whole car industry belongs to it."

Then Birmingham was "a rugby team's bath after they've let the water out" – that is, "a ring of scum round the empty centre". Also, there was "not a single restaurant you would actually choose to eat in unless your children's lives were at stake".

Later it was the turn of the Welsh. When asked why he had put a 3D plastic map of Wales in a microwave and turned it on, he said: "I put Wales in there because Scotland wouldn't fit."

According to friends, Clarkson was much the same at home. He would entertain vegetarians, but if they come round to his house, they have to eat meat stew like everyone else. If they want to eat

22

leaves, they can do it at home, he said. And he is an unrepentant smoker. Eschewing low-tar brands, he smokes Marlboro.

"I like a proper heterosexual cigarette and Marlboro is like red meat on a stick," he said. "Food is really a prelude to smoking – a bit like sex. You have to go through the whole procedure just so you'll enjoy a fag more than if you hadn't done it."

He also loved Budweiser beer.

"It's the only thing the Americans do better than us," he said. "They make good cars but great beer. I can't stand all that real-ale stuff – Old Man's Underpants, the stuff with twigs and old soil in it."

Clarkson was perfectly in tune with the laddism of the mid-1990s. It was the era of *Loaded* magazine and *Men Behaving Badly* on the TV. And Jeremy was definitely one of the lads.

Chapter Four – Making Hay While the Sun Shines

In 1996, Clarkson became a columnist on the *Sun*. The paper introduced him to their readers with "twenty things you never knew about the craziest car critic of them all". These included getting Noel Edmonds to stand in for him when his 6ft 5in-frame would not fit into a car.

"We were filming in a Ford GT40," he said, "and we found out that I was nine inches too tall to get into it. So I rang Noel Edmonds and told him, 'You're a short-arse, so can you do this for us?' And he did."

Although he gets fan mail from lovelorn women, the paper said, Jeremy reckons he is the world's most unlikely pin-up.

"My stomach is the size of a spacehopper," he said. "I weigh sixteen stone and my teeth are yellow from smoking far too much."

He admitted that he would nick cars if he wasn't rich. "If I was a fourteen-year-old kid brought up on a council estate in Doncaster," he said, "and stood no chance of getting a job, then, yeah, I'd nick cars. I'd be reversing into Dixons every night."

By then Emily had started to walk, so he said he had converted a lawnmower into a go-kart for her.

He admitted to driving 186 mph in a Lamborghini Countach. Terrified by the experience, he vowed never to drive faster than 150 mph in future. And he thought that buying personalized number

24

plates was a "filthy nouveau thing to do", but wouldn't mind having some.

"I'd like an amusing one such as DEV1L or PEN1S or, best of all, ORG45M," he said.

He also admitted that he had no idea how a car worked.

"If somebody told me to change the plugs I'd be looking in the boot," he said. On the other hand: "I know which one to drive if you want to pull the birds."

By then Clarkson was driving a Volvo 850R and a Jaguar XJ6, which had also made his Hot 100. But he had given away his beloved Escort Cosworth – another Hot 100 car – as a prize in a competition.

Though he was now writing for Britain's biggest-selling daily paper, he admitted to being a "crap reporter" on the *Rotherham Advertiser*.

"The worst time was when I got slung out of an inquest for laughing at the evidence, which wasn't funny," he said.

Ultimately, he found cars sexy, but no substitute for women.

"There's no swelling when I climb into car," he said, "unlike if I was, say, climbing into Claudia Schiffer. And driving a Ferrari isn't as good as bedding Kate Moss – but it's probably not far off."

This was exactly what *Sun* readers wanted.

Clarkson has a strong line in sexual imagery. When the Ford Ka appeared on *Top Gear* he said: "So the question is, if you drive this, will people want to have your babies or will they laugh in your face."

He aimed his remarks specifically at a small band of enthusiasts.

"These petrol heads want the wind in their hair and exhausts like drain pipes," he said. "They want looks that can snap knicker elastic at fifty paces, sounds that can drown out Guns N' Roses, and power."

But sex was not the only thing on his mind. He picked up images from far and wide. Aston Martin's Vantage – another Hot 100 – was "as brutal as a dockers' boozer, yet… as civilized as an E M Forster heroine".

Talking of Jaguars, he said: "People say there's not much space in there, that you're hemmed in, but I think it makes you feel very cosy and safe". Asked whether this was like being in a cockpit, he said: "No, more like being in a little study with a wood-burning stove. There should be a few books on the walls."

Clarkson was now coining it. Despite his oft-stated aversion to the countryside, he moved with his family to a Georgian mansion in the Cotswolds – a six-acre estate outside Chipping Norton that had formerly belonged to billionaire businessman David Sainsbury – though they kept a flat in London. He claimed he had bought the flat overlooking the Harbour Club in Chelsea so that he could gawp at Princess Diana who used the gym there.

"I was a big Diana fan," he said. "Then, two weeks after I moved in, she got in a car with a drunken Frenchman and that was the end of that."

By then, another child was on its way. This was his son Finlo. The name came from the Isle of Man, where Francie was born and brought up.

In 1996, he released the video *Clarkson: Unleashed on Cars*. It featured "everything he can't do on TV". This included firing a Nissan Sunny from a medieval catapult and driving a Volvo into a tree.

Next he started work on a series provisionally entitled *Jeremy Clarkson Unlimited*. This wouldn't just feature cars, but also power-boats, helicopters and the like – "if it rolls, floats, flies, shoots a bullet, runs on high explosive or gasoline, then we feature it," he said. He wanted to call the series *Big Boys' Toys*.

Clarkson was so much in demand he was even asked to present *Gladiators*. He thought it was a joke. The Gladiators are super fit, while "I'm as fat as a hippopotamus," he said, dubbing himself the "Lardiator". Thus he passed up the opportunity to work with Ulrika Jonsson.

Even so, he now had the money to buy a Ferrari – a red one. "You pick up birds in a Ferrari – you just do," he said.

But there was a downside to driving a Ferrari, he conceded. While most people thought you were flash and gave you the thumbs up, others dismissed you as a "dickhead" or a "wanker". Clarkson was adamant though. He had worked seven days a week for ten years to earn his Ferrari. However, an Austin Maestro and a Citroen Passat were seen in his driveway. They belonged to the cleaner and the nanny.

In the garage were two Sega Rally arcade machines that Francie bought him for his birthday. On them two people can race a Lancia Delta Integrale or a Toyota Celica GT4 on a choice of rally circuits. The Sega Rally machines gave him an opportunity to experiment with drink driving and he found that even after drinking just one glass of wine he could get nowhere near his top score.

"After two bottles of wine, and some sloe vodka, I'm all over the place," he said. "Once, I was so drunk that I was nearly half a second off the pace. And on another occasion, on the forest stage, I actually fell asleep."

It was, he said, almost as much fun as the Ferrari. But while he sped around the virtual test circuits drunk or sober, he did not do so on the open roads. Clarkson was inordinately proud of his clean driving licence.

In 1997, Clarkson and fellow *Top Gear* presenter, bike specialist Steve Berry began trading insults on air.

"We give each other a load of stick when we're working together," said Berry. "He was taking the mick out of me on TV the other day so I returned the compliment. I said on air, 'The heaviest part of any car is the engine – unless of course Jeremy is driving it because, let's face it, he's a bit of a porker.'"

This was passed off as a bit of boys' banter. But things got serious when Berry unleashed an astonishing attack on Clarkson in the *News of the World*.

"I wake up each morning hoping that Jeremy will disappear down a big hole in the ground," he said. "There's nothing about him that I

28

like. He dresses appallingly, likes long-haired seventies monster rock bands – and he's got the worst hairstyle in Britain since Kevin Keegan stopped having that terrible perm."

He also tried to trash Clarkson's bad-boy image.

"He's just a middle-class boy who's a bit sad," Berry said. "His antics at school amount to nothing more than Bunteresque public schoolboy japes... making apple pie beds for the housemaster, refusing to fag for the sixth formers and smoking cigarettes behind the dorm."

Berry himself was brought up on a Manchester council estate. "Where I come from bad behaviour is joy-riding and dealing heroin, cocaine and Ecstasy," said Berry. "And as for his boasts with girls, I bet if one had come on to Jeremy when he was at school, he'd have run a mile."

While Clarkson got a lot of hate mail, Berry claimed to get letters from woman who wanted him to father their children, and he could not wait for Clarkson to leave the show.

Clarkson was in America when the story broke.

"I'm shocked by this," he said. "There has never been anything to provoke this sort of outburst. I can't think what I've done to offend Steve in this way. I never realized he didn't like me."

Berry had a video, *Berry on Bikes*, out at the time, which may have had something to do with his out. But it did nothing to dent the Clarkson carapace. BBC Two immediately commissioned *Jeremy Clarkson's Extreme Machines*, a six-part series where he took rides on jet planes, powerboats, yachts, helicopters, snowmobiles and even combine harvesters and supertankers. In it, he put himself to the test. He was violently sick in the cockpit of a US Air Force F-15, due the effects of g-force. When the jet fighter and landed and he got out, he collapsed.

"It's the first time in my life I've been lost for words," he said.

A swamp buggy capsized in Florida, dumping Clarkson and his crew in the alligator-infested waters, and they lost all their equipment. And sound-man Murray Clarke had a heart attack that put him in hospital for three months when they scaled the side of a supertanker at sea.

"I'm just glad to get back without anyone being killed," Clarkson said when the show was over. And he claimed no credit for his courage.

"I'm Mr Timid, who even holds on to the banister when walking downstairs," he said. "On *Top Gear* we're middle-aged men with families who arrive at the office saying: 'It was great last night. Went home, had supper in front of the telly and was in bed by eleven'."

Francie confirmed that, at home, Clarkson was now a family man who was good with the kids. He was very "Middle England" and even admitted to listening to BBC Radio Two, though he found that, in the car, if he put on a CD of James Bond theme tunes, he got home quicker.

Despite his domestic arrangements his Jack-the-Lad image was fixed in the public's mind. Asked what he would do if he were world leader – after getting rid of Switzerland and America – he said he would get rid of all the bus lanes in the world. He also suggested taxing bicycles for hogging a third of the road and called their riders banana-heads, weird beards and – worst of all – vegetarians. But in 1998, one of his own newspapers, the *Sunday Times*, outed him as a closet cyclist.

"It is a terrible and unexpected shock," said Quentin Willson, a co-presenter of *Top Gear* and a close family friend of the Clarkson's. "He has never once mentioned owning a bike to me. Perhaps he's a budding environmentalist – think of our ratings!"

Forced out into the open, Clarkson confessed to owning and riding a grey, twenty-one-gear Raleigh mountain bike with road-going tyres. It was not on his Hot 100.

Though he had been cycling five miles a day for a month, he said that this had nothing to do with the environment, but rather his weight.

"I was recently described as looking like Stephen Fry's older, fatter sister," he said. "Now I'm lithe, like a racing snake."

A gang of youth in a souped-up Peugeot who passed him when he was out pedalling were not impressed.

"One of them leaned out of the window and suggested that my seed fell on fallow ground," he said. "When they realized who I was they turned round and shouted the same thing but inserted the word 'turncoat' in front of it."

Colleagues on the *Sunday Times* teased him about "greening". In a recent column he had revealed that he was about to buy a Mercedes estate car.

"I am tempted by the diesel, simply because it is the gutsiest of the lot, but diesel fumes kill people, so maybe I will do the world a favour and stick with petrol," he wrote.

He had also described the English countryside as "pretty" and in *Jeremy Clarkson's Hot 100: Cars that Make You Go PHWOAR!*, he recommended modern Ferraris over older models partly because "on-board computers make them more fuel efficient – and new materials make them quieter". On the up side, he had already made fourth FHM's list of worst dressed men in Britain behind Chris Evans, Bob Geldof and Paul Gascoigne – distinguished company, you will agree.

But for Francie, there was no hope.

"To be frank, his behaviour is getting worse, not better," she said. "He has started scouring the country for beef on the bone" – then banned after the outbreak of mad cow disease – "and he has a loathing for anything green."

Further pratfalls faced Clarkson. At the premiere of Steve Coogan's show *The Man Who Thinks He's It*, he approached Oxfordshire neighbour Kate Moss and said: "Hi, I'm Jeremy Clarkson, I do *Top Gear*."

Confused, Kate asked: "Are you trying to sell me drugs?"

It was a blow to his ego that she did not know who he was. But did it not dent his ardour. A month later, he told the *Sunday Mirror* that he would like to take her for a test drive.

Next Clarkson was in trouble for saying that people who rode scooters were homosexual. Then the Korean car-maker Hyundai got the hump when he said that the designers of their "ugly" XG had obviously been too busy eating dogs to style their cars properly. Hyundai promptly complained to BBC Director General John Birt, while Clarkson made a bad situation worst at the Motor Show.

"I'm afraid the following day I poured petrol on the fire by advising visitors who had brought dogs to the show not to walk them past the Hyundai stand. They'll sprinkle some ketchup on the poor thing's back… and the next thing you know you'll have an empty lead," Clarkson said.

He was told to make no more references to dogs.

"So, no mention then of Rover and how it escaped the Nazi blitz only to be bought by the Germans and closed down that way," he wrote. "No telling the crowds how it's a dog-eat-dog world out there, and absolutely no way of saying Hyundai had been barking up the wrong tree with the hideous XG."

Chapter Five – Chatty Man

The Korean dog furore took place at a time when Clarkson had been asked to host a chat show on BBC Two. Initially Clarkson had refused, pointing out that "Barry Norman would never do a programme on cookery and that Keith Floyd is no threat to Alan Titchmarsh". He said he was a car man and could talk of nothing else. But the controller of BBC Two summoned him for lunch.

"All the way down to London I practised saying no over and over, in a wide variety of new and interesting ways," he said. "By the time I'd parked, I was ready to burst into the restaurant and say: 'Mark, I'd rather gouge my eyes out with a typewriter. I'd rather dance naked in Covent Garden. I'd rather sell my children into white slavery. I cannot do it and I will not do it. But since I'm here, I'll start with the melon boat.'"

A month later, he was filming a pilot which, he said, was "the worst forty minutes of television ever committed to tape". Clarkson then said he tried again to get out of doing the chat show. He told the BBC that he was shy, that he had a coke habit, that he had "a string of affairs with girls aged nine".

Before, on television, he had always had a prop – be it a Lamborghini or an aircraft carrier. Now he was on his own, in a studio, in a suit. And he perspired.

"It's hard to be witty and fast when your back is like the Atlantic," he said.

But Clarkson was riding high. The BBC had recently aired the five-part series *Top Gear Waterworld*, where he and other presenters went messing about in boats. Back in 1980, Clarkson had taken a course to get a Master Mariner's certificate when the family bought a motor cruiser in the South of France. He once said that he preferred boats to cars. On the water, there are no speed limits and you can drink and drive, though it is not a good idea to be paralytic, he said.

This gave him the confidence to think that the chat show might just work. He would ask Gary Barlow why he had never driven his car into a swimming pool and he figured there must be other people would wanted to nuke America or would nod when he explained why all Greek men pretend to be homosexual.

But then he realized how much trouble his remarks about scooter-riding homosexuals and dog-eating Koreans had caused. With him hosting a chat show, his critics would declare open season. So either he would have to carry on regardless – and dig a moat around his house, or he would have change tack and say that cricket was interesting and that he was always wanted to be a freemason. The choice was terrifying.

"There's only one cure," he wrote in his column in the *Sunday Times*. "It's called Going to Barbados For A Couple Of Months And Hiding Behind A Palm Tree. Bye."

When *Clarkson* aired in November 1998, he reckoned that half the audience wanted it to fail. But his personality prevailed – and he was now earning something in the region of £500,000 a year. The show ran for two years – twenty-seven episodes in all.

With this and his commitments to *Top Gear*, Clarkson had precious little time at home. Nevertheless, he taught the children to drive almost as soon as they could walk. On their private estate they were also protected from the pressures of their father's fame. Meanwhile Francie was pregnant again and gave birth to another daughter, Katya.

Mostly he was based in the flat in London. The countryside could wait until he was retired, he said. Although he promised Francie that he worked late, went to bed early and lived on takeaways, it was soon clear from the credit-card bills that he was out every night. He was enjoying every minute of being back in town.

With his fame hitting new heights, young women were eager to flirt with him. Francie said she was not jealous, rather she was proud to be with a man who was in demand.

Instead of sitting back and enjoying his fame, he continued working seven days a week. He knew that fame was fragile and he had to make the best of it while it lasted. He figured that anyone who loved cars and could write a script could do his job. Besides, a great many people were out for his scalp. He only had to look at his mail to confirm that.

While Clarkson continued to insist that *Top Gear* was nothing more than "half an hour of entertainment fluff" which had no effect on car sales, he was blamed for a slump in the demand for jeans.

"Fashion gurus say that young people don't want to be associated with 'old gits' like me and black the catastrophic thirteen per cent fall in jeans sales on what's been christened the Jeremy Clarkson Effect," he told the *Sun*. "This is fantastic. Most people strive all their lives to get a miserable OBE or a so-what knighthood. And without even trying, I get my own 'effect'."

Then in 1999, Clarkson shocked his fans by suddenly announcing that he was leaving *Top Gear*.

"I'd taken *Top Gear* as far as I could," he said. "I decided it was time for a change."

He had been in discussion with BBC bosses about new programmes, particularly documentaries. During his ten years on the show he had driven every new car that came onto the market, except the Mitsubishi Carisma, which he said was "no great loss". He also claimed that he had never pranged any car he tested "unlike Quentin Willson".

He wrote in *Top Gear* magazine: "I will, of course, carry on writing for this magazine, and there's always Mr Murdoch to stand bravely between my front door and the wolf, but already I'm starting to miss *Top Gear*. I miss the banter with Quentin and Tiff, as we sniggered about Steve Berry and what he's crashed that week. I miss Vicki's eyes and her ability to bring sex into absolutely everything."

On his departure, he could not resist taking another swipe at Birmingham, calling it "the armpit that masquerades as Britain's second city". *Top Gear* was based in the BBC's Pebble Mill studios there. The King's Heath suburb was compared to a Columbian town recently devastated by an earthquake – "only worse".

"In seven days, God created heaven and earth and then, just to keep his oppo amused, he let Beelzebub do Birmingham," he said.

Clarkson was going to be a hard act to follow. Before he had joined the show its viewing figures were in the hundreds of thousands. By 1999, it had topped six million.

James May, he said, was being touted as his replacement, "lured by the promise of untold riches, of motor industry obsequiousness on a biblical scale and of bathing in an intoxicating mix of public adulation and Dom Perignon. But he has not considered that his drive from England to Pebble Mill will mean getting through King's Heath."

At the same time, Clarkson had managed to get himself embroiled in politics after attacking Deputy Prime Minister and Transport Secretary John Prescott's White Paper that sought to reduce pollution and congestion by encouraging commuters to use public transport. Clarkson said that people would always prefer the car over public transport because in the "car you can sing, shout, do what you want. You can't do this on trains – you catch diseases on trains". Prescott's White Paper, he said was "being used as lavatory paper in Phoney Tony's downstairs loo".

Shadow Chancellor Francis Maude said the Tories would be interested in getting together with him to discuss these matters. Clarkson was outraged by the suggestion. He was no Tory puppet and thought that the Conservatives were trying to cash in on his popularity. He refused to meet them and threatened to shoot whoever had come up with the idea. Clarkson had little time for politicians.

More controversy followed. When Clarkson said that paella was made from rice and whatever happened to be in your bin, the *Independent* accused him of being racist. At least, that was his version of the story. In fact, the paper had quoted Clarkson saying: "Spain in the afternoon is closed. This is because the Spanish go for a nap. They even have a word for it – siesta. Of course, we have two words for it: lazy and bastard."

His producer, Elaine Bedell, defended him saying they had produced some "very funny television". He was also condemned for being homophobic for describing certain cars as gay. Drugs should be legalized because "no one breaks into your home because they need funds for music lessons". The police were "trimming their moustaches to look good on next week's edition of *Police. Stop. Kill.*, while the Crown Prosecution Service were busy sorting out the video rights.

Clarkson began to form a double act with fellow *Sunday Times* columnist A A Gill. Travelling to Cheshire with him, Gill said: "For a place where the showroom is a cathedral of pilgrimage and the double garage a family chapel, Clarkson is the Second Coming. People don't mob him so much as genuflect to him... They sway after him in ecstatic Hare Krishna lines, chanting: 'Jezza, Jezza, Jezza, Jezza, Clarkson, Clarkson, Jezza, Jezza'." In the face of such adulation, all Gill could do was whisper that Clarkson was gay.

Nevertheless, girls asked him to autograph their thighs with mascara. One asked: "Can you put, 'To a 911 driver with love.'"

Gill and Clarkson ended up playing golf for the first time. Clarkson admitted to liking the game, but said to take it up, he would have to pretend to his wife that he had a mistress and hide his kit in friend's home.

Later Gill and Clarkson teamed up again to travel to Iceland, America, the Greek island of Mykonos, largely a gay resort, and, daringly, to Iraq.

In 2000, the BBC gave him a six-part series called *Clarkson's Car Years* where he looked at the rise and fall of the supercar, why people like British sports cars, how Japan took over the world's car manufacturing and the decline of the British car industry. During the filming, one of the researchers managed to crash a £136,000 Lamborghini Diablo into the crash barriers in London's Park Lane. At first Clarkson was "incandescent with rage". But later, he said: "When the researcher realizes the enormity of what he's done, he'll be a hero. He's crashed. A Lamborghini. On Park Lane. And that's fantastic. His colleagues are green with envy. They were talking about their crashes and one was forced to admit his best was 'falling off a moped in Wardour Street'. We're thinking of sacking him instead."

That December, his chat show was cancelled after three series.

"It wasn't my thing," Clarkson admitted. "The first series was pretty awful and I was getting better, but I prefer being outdoors in a pair of jeans."

Having your own chat show as just part of being an all-round TV personality.

"Alan Titchmarsh did a chat show for a while, Carol Smillie did a chat show for a while, I did a chat show for a while," he said. "But the fact is Titchmarsh is a gardener, Carol Smillie is a decorator and I'm a car journalist.

The celebrity pow-wows were not his thing. Soon he had flung away his suit and was clad in his old attire. In 2001, the BBC aired Clarkson's six-part series *Speed* which examined why some people like speed and others don't and looked at the history of fast vehicles including aeroplanes, boats, car, roller coasters and bobsleds. He topped 215 mph on the Salt Lakes of Utah and interviewed racing drivers, test pilots, sky divers, speed skiers and other dare devils.

"I know that half the people tuning in to *Speed* will be doing so just to see me make a fool of myself and they won't be disappointed," he said. "We had a series of disasters and I've never been as genuinely frightened as I was doing this. People have been killed going down bobsleigh runs and when I asked if I was insured people just laughed at me. Then about halfway down, doing 80 mph, the serotonin in my brain kicked in and I froze with fear. After the run when they wanted me to comment on how I felt I couldn't speak."

Worse came when he flew with the British pilots of the Empire Test School in Wiltshire. "I was taken up to 42,000 feet and then they stall the engine so you go into freefall for about 20,000 feet. You fall axle over axle and I was explosively sick everywhere," he said. "I felt dreadful and I was in a fair amount of pain. I didn't feel much better when we landed either or for about three days afterwards and I really wouldn't want to repeat the experience."

But he was not the only one to suffer. In the first episode, he took his sixty-five-year-old mum on a roller coaster.

"We wanted to do a test on the Big One roller-coaster at Blackpool Pleasure Beach and I thought, 'Who can I get to do this? I know, I'll get my mum'," he said. "Of course, she hated the idea, and she hated the whole experience, but I bunged her pounds 100 and she was OK with that."

And he had a clear eye for what the audience wanted from him.

"While the show aimed to be an investigation of how fast we can go and how much faster we will go in future, I also know there will be people watching who hate me and are only waiting to see me suffer," he said. "There are plenty of those, believe me."

Thanks to the series, he bought himself a decommissioned Lightning jet fighter as an ornament for his Oxfordshire garden, much to the chagrin of Francie. It was later removed on orders of the local council.

Clarkson's feud with Piers Morgan, then editor of the *Daily Mirror*, began in 2000, when the *Mirror* were given pictures of Clarkson in a clinch with Elaine Bedell, the producer of his chat show. Morgan said that he and Clarkson had always got on pretty well, so he phoned Jeremy to suggest he made a joke out of it. However, Morgan pointed out that Clarkson was writing a column in the *Sun*, "which he signed up for after virtually promising me he'd do it in the *Mirror*. So I hardly owe him any favours."

Clarkson insisted that he and Bedell were not doing anything, and claimed he was not capable of having an affair. "You can ask my wife," he said. "I'm not physically capable. I'm telling you this so you can see how ridiculous these pictures are."

But Morgan would not relent. He ran the pictures the following day under the headline 'We are colleagues who were just fooling around'.

The paper reported: "The eighteen-stone, 6ft 5in host was first spotted with petite Elaine at the swish Pharmacy restaurant in Notting Hill. They enjoyed a ninety-minute lunch before walking hand in hand to Jeremy's current car, a Honda HRV advertised by its Japanese makers as 'The Joy Machine', before heading back to work in White City.

"An onlooker who saw them when they stopped off said: 'They were kissing in the front seats. A little old lady was walking past and peered through the windscreen. When she saw what they were doing, her face lit up.'"

Clarkson protested that their relationship was purely platonic. "If you are someone like me and you are having an affair you wouldn't do it in one of the most famous restaurants in London which has a completely glass front exterior."

At the time, the Clarkson's marriage was reckoned to be one of the most solid in television.

"I don't know how Francie puts up with me," he said. "But she's caring and kind and just rolls her eyes at my raving views on things."

Francie admitted that she was irritated by his laddish ways. "He sings in the bath, leaves cigarette ends by the side of the sink and never replaces the loo roll," she said.

Two years later Clarkson and Francie met at a bash in Claridge's where they berated Morgan for running the pictures. Wishing to avoid a row, Morgan apologized. But three years later, he ran more pictures of Clarkson in a clinch with Bedell under the headline: 'Oh Jeremy! – Three years after we last caught him, Clarkson is back canoodling with his boss'.

This time Morgan did not call Clarkson for an explanation, but they met three weeks later on the last flight of Concorde. After a robust exchange of views Clarkson emptied a glass of water in Morgan's lap.

Clarkson also had a long running feud with Janet Street-Porter. She kept him on her "Shit List", while he said that he hoped wolves were re-introduced to the country so they would eat the "rambling queen".

That summer the five part series *Meet the Neighbours* aired. In it Clarkson took an E-Type Jaguar on a 20,000-mile road trip around France, Belgium and the Netherlands, Germany, Spain and Italy, describing how the inhabitants' lifestyles differed from those enjoyed in Britain. Playing the Little Englander, he posed the vital questions "are the Dutch a bunch of dope smoking pornographers?"; "Do the Germans have a sense of humour?" and "Is there anything interesting about the Belgians?" Poking fun at "Johnny Foreigner", he described the French as a bunch of "onion selling ne'er-do-wells" and tried to find out why they seem to appear so smug – but ended up rather liking them.

Chapter Six – Top Gear Goes Global

Three years after quitting *Top Gear*, Clarkson returned like the Terminator. The show had been off the air for a year and the show's other presenters Quentin Willson, Tiff Needell and Vicki Butler-Henderson had jumped ship for *Fifth Gear* on Channel Five.

"It's a compliment that the BBC are so afraid of losing ratings to us they've lured my old co-host out of semi-retirement from his toe-curling chat show," said Willson.

It was reported that Clarkson was given a £1-million deal to front the new show and BBC Two billed him as "bigger, bolder and ruder than ever before". The show itself was given a complete makeover. Clarkson was bored with reviewing solid, middle of the range cars. They were all much the same and he could not think of anything to say about them. So the new *Top Gear* would be a studio-based show where they would talk about cars. Outside they would have a test track outside where they could drive fast.

The show would now be an hour long, rather than thirty minutes. It would be topical, made only a few days before it aired. They would also be very picky about which cars appeared on the show. Each would have to be special and different. This was not to be the run-of-the-mill consumer show that the original *Top Gear* had set out to be.

The show was relocated to Dunsfold Aerodrome. The hanger there was used as a studio and the runways and taxiways were used as a test track, where cars were put through their paces by Clarkson and his two co-presenters, Richard Hammond and Jason Dawe, replaced by James May after the first series, along with the mute helmeted racing driver known only as "The Stig". As well as car reviews, the show also featured various themed segments and celebrity guests. Then there were specials that had the three presenters driving across Africa or racing to the North Pole. Spin-offs included DVDs, music compilations and live shows.

"Since we changed *Top Gear*, I don't have to drive the boring cars," said Clarkson. "People say 'I'm thinking of buying a Renault Clio, what's it like?' I haven't got a clue. I've no idea. Watch Channel Five, I'm sure they'll tell you," he said, taking a swing at his former colleagues.

Also in 2002, Clarkson was also invited to appear on the show *Great Britons*, which sought to discover who people thought was the greatest Briton who ever lived. He chose to champion the Victorian engineer Isambard Kingdom Brunel, who built the Great Western Railway and designed the *Great Western* steamship to carry passengers on from Bristol to America.

Showing a less laddish side, Clarkson said of Brunel: "He built modern Britain and, as modern Britain built the world, Brunel built the world."

Thanks to Clarkson, Brunel came second, ahead of Cromwell, Darwin, Princess Diana, Elizabeth I, John Lennon, Nelson, Newton and Shakespeare. He was only beaten by Winston Churchill championed by Mo Mowlam. Ever controversial, Clarkson dismissed Churchill as "just a drunk who happened to be in the right place at the right time".

Clarkson went on to back Brunel's biennial festival in Swindon in 2006. In his ringing endorsement, Clarkson said: "Darwin told us where we came from, but it was Brunel who took us to where we wanted to go."

The following year, he present the documentary *The Victoria Cross*: *For Valour* which examined the history of the Victoria Cross, and followed the story of one of the 1,354 men who were awarded it – namely Major Robert Henry Cain, who received it for his courage during the battle for Arnhem in September 1944. At the end of the programme it was revealed that Major Cain was Francie's father. Apparently he had died in 1978 without ever telling his daughter of his award.

While his championing of Brunel and Major Cain revealed a more mature side to Clarkson, his first love was still cars. He became host of "MPH '03", billed as "a motor show with a difference". According to Clarkson, conventional motor shows were pretty much dead in the UK.

"The notion of turning up and mooching around in a huge crowd and occasionally catching a glimpse of a wheel of a car you could see outside anyway seems a bit stupid," he said. "MPH '03 is where you can look at the more exciting cars on stands but then there's a proper indoor racetrack to go in, sit down and watch cars going quickly. Cars are supposed to move, that's what they're meant to do.

It's the future of motor shows. If we get round without a crash a day, I'll be astonished."

Held at London's Earls Court and the NEC in Birmingham, it showed off supercars. From 2011, the MPH show was re-launched as "Top Gear Live." This began to tour and has been in twenty-eight cities in twenty-two countries on four continents. There have been 301 performances seen by 1.8 million fans so far. *Top Gear* already aired worldwide via the BBC's overseas channels and other outlets, and the format was sold to Australia, Russia, the US and Korea, who began to make their own version of the show. *Top Gear* had gone global.

Clarkson increased his television footprint further by agreeing to take part in *What Not to Wear* with style gurus Trinny Woodall and Susannah Constantine. He had also made their shortlist of the twenty World's Worst Dressed.

"They said all my clothes were rubbish and that my legs were too long. How can legs be too long?" he said. "And how can a pair of Levis be rubbish? But apparently they were, so they dragged me, by my hair, around London making me try on upside-down trousers and shirts that won't tuck in so now I look like a contestant on *Who Wants to be a Millionaire?*"

But Clarkson got his own back in his column in the *Sunday Times*.

"After filming each day, Susannah would climb into her Rover 75 and go home," he wrote. "Did you catch that? She'd climb into her Rover 75 and go home. Susannah, sweetie, how can you be so bothered about your appearance if you're prepared to drive round in a vicar's elbow patch? No, don't argue. The Rover 75 is as last week as one of Alan Hansen's shirts."

By series three of the revamped *Top Gear* Clarkson was getting into his stride and set out to find out whether a Toyota Hilux pickup was really indestructible. He took a second-hand vehicle, bounced it down some stone steps, scrapped it pass the corner of a wall, ran it into a tree, parked in on a boat ramp where the tide would cover it and eventually washed it away. Then he smashed it though a hut, dropped a caravan on it, hit with a wrecking ball, set fire to it – and it kept on going. In the next episode, James May put it on top of a tower block that was then demolished with high explosives. Still it survived.

There were, of course, complaints. The BBC had to pay £250 compensation to the parish council of Churchill in Somerset for abusing their tree. Clarkson was unrepentant.

"The parish council is funded by central government, which is funded by me, so it's my tree," he said. "Anyway, there was no damage."

Clarkson then appeared on *Who Do You Think You Are?* At first he dismissed genealogy as "too boring to bother with".

"Take the Clarkson name back to its Yorkshire roots and they all come from within a few miles of each other," he said. "I'm the product of two hundred years of interbreeding – I'm surprised I haven't got one eye!"

But then he discovered his link to glass-maker John Kilner. This piqued his interest.

"Selfishly, I'm quite keen to find out what happened to the money," he said. "Is there somewhere a dusty piece of paper that says Jeremy Clarkson is owed £48 billion?"

There wasn't, but Clarkson was thrilled to know that his ancestors had played a part in the growth of the British Empire – "the most extraordinary superpower the world has ever seen". The Kilner company had its own railway sidings and a shipping fleet that carried its products to the four corners of the globe.

Next Clarkson appeared on *Parkinson* and talked eloquently about the demise of Concorde. It was a machine, he said, that had "soul" – like the Toyota Hilux he and James May had done so much damage to.

"No car, however, gets close to the aching sadness I feel for Concorde," he wrote. "Next time I'm passing Heathrow, in the season of goodwill, I may drop in and buy it some soup."

He went on to develop these ideas in the book *I Know You Got Soul* which included such a diverse selection of soulful items as the flying boat, the AK47, the Zeppelin, the satellite dish on Goonhilly Down, Japan's doomed battleship *Yamato* and the *Millennium Falcon* from *Star Wars*.

The re-launch of *Top Gear* and his subsidiary work made Clarkson a wealthy man and he bought a holiday home on the Isle of Man, where residents enjoyed certain tax benefits. Though ostensibly part of the establishment, Clarkson continued to be a thorn in the side of the environmental lobby. To launch series six, he, James May and

Richard Hammond staged a publicity stunt at Hammersmith bus depot.

Clarkson explained: "Having been told by various pressure groups to be more environmentally friendly, we decided to support Greenpeace who this week broke into the Land Rover factory and chained themselves to the production line. We agreed that enormous, gas-guzzling vehicles clogging up the city streets with only one person on board was stupid... so we went to Hammersmith and handcuffed ourselves to the worst offender – a bus."

As a result, the bus driver asked for their autographs.

"Sadly, it wasn't a very effective protest," said Clarkson, "partly because the only handcuffs we could find were from Ann Summers, partly because we locked ourselves to a bus that was out of service and partly because, when the police came, we gave in and went to the pub."

The whole thing was filmed, of course, for *Top Gear*. Transport for London complained to the Broadcasting Standards Council, saying that they had caused "a considerable amount of disruption," while the Film Office said: "Clowns like him put other people's jobs at risk" and fired off an official complaint to the BBC. Not that Clarkson was bothered. A journalist from the *Independent* who phoned his home reported: "His wife told me that he was busy and didn't feel like talking about work at the weekend."

He also took another swing at cyclists with his five handy hints for those setting out on a bike for the first time in the *Sun*. They were: "Do not cruise through red lights. Because if I'm coming the other way, I will run you down, for fun. Do not pull up at junctions in front of a line of traffic. Because if I'm behind you, I will set off at normal speed and you will be crushed under my wheels. Do not wear Lycra shorts unless you are Kate Moss. I do not wish to cruise down the road looking at your meat and two veg. Do not, ever, swear at or curse people in cars or trucks. You are a guest on roads that are paid for by motorists so if we cut you up, shut up. Do not wear a helmet. It makes you look ridiculous."

For once, the *Guardian* agreed. The paper said cyclists taking to the road after the 7/7 London underground and bus bombings should "beware of a large, intemperate man with no obvious sense of irony driving a very fast car".

"How many children or elderly people have been knocked down by wizened, *Guardian*-reading, muesli freaks in figure-hugging Lycra?" Clarkson asked.

Chapter Seven – Winning the War of Words

Clarkson still had his serious side. In 2005, he and A A Gill went to Iraq. Realizing the dangers, Clarkson decided not to take a TV crew with him. Instead he would recruit one when he got there. His intention was, he said, to "get Bin Laden to be our Star In A Reasonably Priced Car!"

The *Sun*'s TV editor Sara Nathan caught up with Clarkson as he was packing: "Bog roll, malaria tablets, diarrhoea tablets and… oh yes, a bit of body armour."

Travelling from Basra to Baghdad, the Hercules transporter they were flying on was targeted three times by rocket-propelled grenades. Then the compound where they were staying in was mortared. There he filmed a segment for *Top Gear* while cowering in the back of an armoured Land Rover.

"I wasn't at the wheel but I directed the piece," he said. "It might be a bit shaky –that will be the nerves. Hopefully we will use it on the show." On his return, he said: "I was away for a few days but it felt like three months. I'm just relieved to be back home in one piece – with no holes in me."

For once, he had given the BBC's health and safety officers the slip. "On *Top Gear*, we refer to the Health and Safety people as the PPD. The Programme Prevention Department," he said.

It had long been the bane of his existence.

"Every week, as we filmed my television chat show, food would be spilt on the floor, and every week the recording would have to be stopped so it could be swept away. 'What would happen,' said the man from health and safety, 'if a cameraman were to slip over?' 'Well,' I would reply, 'he'd probably have to stand up again'," he wrote in *The World According to Clarkson.*

After fending off the BBC's "health and safety enthusiasts" to ride a jet ski across Lake Como with wearing a helmet or a life jacket – nor have a squad of trained and very expensive divers on hand – he was shocked to find his Twitter feed jammed up by ordinary members of the public who said he was setting a bad example by not wearing safety equipment. "This made me so angry, my teeth started to itch," he said.

He riled conservationists by driving a 4x4 through a Scottish peat bog. He infuriated the green lobby further by saying: "My wife bought me a patio heater for our anniversary and I've always been a bit nervous of it. Now I know the environmental lot hate them so much I'll burn it 24 hours a day."

When MG Rover collapsed this year and Clarkson wrote: "When I heard the news my first thought was 'Good'." In response, workers hung a banner outside the plant proclaiming an "Anti-Clarkson Campaign".

When Oxford Brookes University decided to award him an honorary degree some three thousand people signed an online petition protesting and, at the award ceremony, he was hit in the face with a pie, later said to be organic. Clarkson's response was: "Great shot." His one complaint was that the meringue was a little too sweet.

"At least they didn't dig my granny up," he told the press, referring to the animal rights campaigners who desecrated the grave of a relative of a Staffordshire farming family rearing guinea pigs for research.

A concerned correspondent to the *Sunday Times* worked out that, if the flan flinger had cooked in the offending pie in an electric oven for one hour and kept it in the refrigerator for a day before delivery, the energy required would have produced 1.92 kilograms of CO_2. For the same amount of CO_2 he could have driven an Aston Martin DB9 for 4.9km, a Land Rover Discovery V8 petrol for 5.4 km, and a Ford Focus for 13.2km.

He ruffled other feathers by saying trains should not stop for people who kill themselves by jumping on to the tracks and declared that he would have the strikers "taken outside and executed in front of their families". The BBC got 20,000 complaints. Ed Miliband called Clarkson's words "disgraceful and disgusting" and neighbour David Cameron merely said they were "silly". Meanwhile the Mexican ambassador objected to *Top Gear*'s characterization of his countrymen as "lazy, feckless, flatulent, overweight, leaning against a fence asleep, looking at a cactus, with a blanket with a hole in the middle as a coat". Co-presenter James May added that Mexican food was "like sick with cheese on it".

But Mexico was just taking is place among Clarkson's least favoured nations. "The problem with France is that, like Wales, it is a very pretty country spoiled only by the people who live there," he said. Asked by a Welshman why he had got in for Wales, he replied: "What with the Germans and Koreans to think about, I honestly haven't time to be hating the Welsh… it's Surrey I hate…if Kent is the garden of England then Surrey is surely the patio. It's shit."

And America? "America may have given the world the space shuttle and, er, condensed milk, but behind the veneer of civilization most Americans barely have the brains to walk on their back legs."

During the Mexican furore it came out that he had taken a super-injunction against his first wife who claimed that they continued their affair while he was married to Francie.

The Independent went to the lengths of drawing up a charge sheet against him. He was, the paper said: "Wanted, for crime against the planet." The specific charge was "causing reckless damage to the environment, hastening global warming". However, the paper had to concede that Clarkson was not a climate-change denier.

"But let's just stop and think for a moment what the consequences might be," he said. "Switzerland loses its skiing resorts? The beach in Miami is washed away? North Carolina gets knocked over by a hurricane? Anything bothering you yet?"

Nevertheless the paper found him "guilty as hell". He was told he should be sent to "an eco-wilderness re-education camp far away from his Chipping Norton home to live as one with nature, Iron John-style for several years, and only readmitted into normal society when fuel cell cars with automatic speed cut-offs are the norm".

It did not stop there. Next was "Wanted, for crimes against common decency", specifically "road-hoggery, threatening behaviour and all-round offensiveness". As a witness for the prosecution, the paper called, of all people, Piers Morgan who said that, at the 2004 British Press Awards, "I made the fatal error of jokily inviting him to punch me on the head, which is precisely what he then did a few hours later." However, most people applauded Clarkson's action and wished he had done it again – harder. The newspaper could only find him "guilty – but not so guilty".

Then there was "Wanted, for crimes against fashion", specifically "flagrant public appearances in the – ugh! – blue-denim garb of everybloke". Clarkson's response: "I live in the middle of the countryside. So long as you can't see my genitals, I consider myself to be well-dressed." Again, with a flagrantly fixed jury, he was found guilty and sentenced to a hundred hours community service as an intern in a Lucie Clayton finishing school.

Things took a more serious turn when censure reached parliament. Naturally Clarkson rose to the challenge.

"A Liberal Democrat MP called Tom Brake, who has the silliest teeth in politics, said he was going to table an early-day motion and drag me to London to watch him doing it," wrote Clarkson. "Now look. I don't want to see anyone's early day motion, least of all a Liberal Democrat's, which would be full of leaf mulch. And I especially don't want to see it on a table. Why can't these people write me a letter saying, 'I don't agree with you'? Why do they have to pie me and make me stand around watching a Liberal with mad teeth doing his number twos? It's beyond comprehension."

Clarkson then discovered Labour's Colin Challen wanted him dead after the environmentalist MP said "sadly we don't have capital punishment in this country" when discussing the *Top Gear* presenter's attitude to the environment. The repost was vigorous.

"Strangely, he's on record as saying he doesn't believe in capital punishment," said Clarkson, "so he doesn't want Peter Sutcliffe dead. He doesn't want Ian Huntley dead. And he thinks Gary Glitter should evade the firing squad. But he does want to see me swinging from the rafters in Wormwood Scrubs. He wants to see the faces of my distraught children on the television news and laugh at my wife as they cut me down and feed my limp, lifeless body to the prison pigs."

As Challen had been elected Clarkson could not write him off as "a complete window-licker... But then again, he does have a beard, he is called Colin..."

Francie constantly warned him that his mouth would get him into trouble.

"He does know," said an old friend. "He doesn't care. He doesn't care what other people think. He is, despite the showbiz connections and career, an absolutely classic Yorkshireman, like Geoff Boycott or Freddie Trueman. You can take him or leave him and he is not even slightly interested in what your decision might be."

Chapter Eight – The Grate and the Good

According the *Daily Express* the "most arrogant, rude and puerile man on TV" was now on his way to becoming a national treasure. It was obviously right that a national treasure should suffer some wear and tear. Clarkson had been diagnosed with osteoarthritis and needed his hip joints replacing with plastic ones. He took this in good part, saying that he had been warned not to lean against radiators in case they melted and that his wife had asked their lawyer to file for divorce because she did not want to be married to a cripple.

Then he suffered two slipped discs. The doctor has ordered him to have six months' total rest and gave him a prescription for painkillers so strong that he spent "half the day wondering whether I'm a horse and the other half answering only to the name Stephen". But when he boasted to Francie that he had managed to present *Top Gear* without an epidural, she stopped speaking to him.

Unbowed, Clarkson turned out with other national treasures – Jeffery Archer, Tony Blair, the Queen, Andrew Lloyd-Webber, Tim Rice, Shirley Bassey, June Whitfield and Marco Pierre White – for Margaret Thatcher's eightieth birthday party at the Mandarin Oriental Hotel near Hyde Park. Later, he attended her funeral alongside the Queen, Tony Blair, Hillary Clinton, Lord Heseltine and Jeffery Archer.

Though he had plainly joined the great and the good, Clarkson still had some implacable enemies. Environmental writer George Monbiot ripped into Clarkson on Jeremy Vine's Radio Two show thus: "I suggest that instead of getting into an overpowered 4x4 and ripping up the countryside, he responds to one of those emails which offers to enhance the size of his manhood." Later Monbiot wrote to Clarkson apologizing. Monbiot had merely strengthened Clarkson's conviction that the Green lobby never listen to the other side of the debate.

"Greenpeace," he said, "has taken a long hard look at the world. It has noted the alarming emergence of Islamic extremism, and the corruption in Africa. It's logged the oppression in Burma and the slaughter in the Middle East. And it has decided that something must be done… about your patio heater."

Ben Stewart of Greenpeace responded: "Clarkson is a class A muppet and absolute plonker. One can only assume that his jeans are restricting his blood-flow. He says things about global warming that are wrong. Also he's said that he has wet dreams about Greenpeace ships turning over. He's best ignored, but that's pretty bad."

Clarkson response was typically brisk. "I do wish these people would take up something useful. Like tearing their own tongues out," he said.

But then Clarkson deliberately set out to annoy. When Gordon Ramsay pipped *Top Gear* to the post at the BAFTA's, Clarkson said: "I hated him on a cellular level. I wanted to stove his head in with a piece of lead piping. I wanted to shave his face off with a linoleum knife and set fire to his Bentley."

He said that being backstage among the presenters and nominees was like being on the set of *Star Wars*. "I'm sure some of the people there had trunks," he said. "I met one judge from *Dragon's Den* wearing make-up so thick he would have needed dynamite to get it off."

Boris Johnson was late for the event. According to Clarkson, he had got lost and blamed Tony Blair. Jordan had to be built by helpers before she appeared in front of the camera, while Peter Andre, "so far as I could tell, was made from plastic".

Clarkson clearly did not enjoy these industry bashes. "I spend half my life at awards ceremonies, losing," he rued. "The number of people who are officially better than me includes pretty well everyone. Even Fred Dibnah, and he's dead."

But then it was much easier to lose that to win. "When you win, you have to look pleased without coming across as smug or arrogant," he said. "Whereas when you lose, you can smile gormlessly and throw your hands up in the air as if to say 'I'm useless.' If you get it right, everyone will want to hug you afterwards and tell you that you're not useless at all. Which is why I spent the post-BAFTA party being massaged by all sorts of pretty girls in very small dresses. Meanwhile, Gordon bloody Ramsay went home all on his own with a useless face on a stick."

Clarkson also began to alienate his neighbours on the Isle of Man. He dubbed local ramblers "sheep killers" and blocked off a centuries old path with barbed wire to prevent "unpleasant and deeply militant dog-walkers" peering in through his kitchen window. The path passed his house was not a right-of-way, but the landowner has historically allowed ramblers access to the coastal path to Langness to enjoy views out over the Irish Sea.

"You have these clots who think they have a God-given right to trample around on somebody else's garden and kill the sheep," said Clarkson. But Manx parliament President Noel Cringle said: "If he is stopping walkers then we need to have words. He should not be doing it."

He upset road-safety campaigners as well as the denizens of Lincolnshire when he admitted driving "fast and recklessly" through the county because it was so boring.

"If JC rockets through your district it is only because it is so dull," he wrote in *Top Gear* magazine.

Lincolnshire had one of Europe's worst death crash rates. Jean Graham, who set up Roadpeace, a support group for crash victims, after her daughter was killed in a smash with a speeding motorist, added: "These remarks are so soul-destroying to the relatives of those who have died."

Clarkson was unrepentant. "We're going through a period when they've got it in for the car," he said. "It's all nonsense. I like these people who are going round defacing speed cameras."

He had even taught his children, then eleven, nine and seven, to drive. Emily had even driven a Porsche.

"It's sensible," he said. "When they pass their driving tests they won't feel the need to go a zillion miles an hour and have all this aggression inside them like all the other teenage monsters on the road."

The police, he said, were "lazy, inefficient, office-bound police, whose response to an extraordinary rise in violent crime is to order more speed cameras". Tony Blair's legacy was "a bus lane on the M4" and the country was "in the hands of overpaid bastards who want to make our lives as miserable as possible".

He defended himself against the charge of yobbishness, saying: "I'm forty-five years old, for heaven's sake, and I have bosoms."

And he was irredeemably bourgeois. "Only last week I was at my children's sports day," he wrote, "and as I lay in the long grass by the river drinking pink champagne and chatting with other media parents, I remember thinking, 'God, I love being middle class.'"

Multiculturalism did not float his board either. "When I go to a dinner party the guests are always white. All my friends have white spouses. And the only diversity in the office where I work is that three of the staff are left-handed. As a result I never meet any black or Asian people. So in this country at least I have no black or Asian friends. Not one." Though he admitted to knowing three Jewish people.

He made these remarks without malice. "Instead of forcing a Pakistani teenager to swear allegiance to the flag and learn English and get some crummy certificate of Britishness from the local mayor," he said, "why not let him be a Pakistani who happens to live in Bradford? Let him go to a Muslim school. Let him support Pakistan when they play England at cricket. Let him be what he wants to be."

Germany still came in for more than its fair share of stick. Reviewing the new Mini – built in Oxford by BMW – he said it was "quintessentially German". The indicators worked like a Nazi salute, miming this with his arm. It had "a sat-nav that only goes to Poland" and "ein fanbelt that will last a thousand years". There were, of course, complaints. German diplomats pointed out that Clarkson would face six years in jail if he had made a Nazi salute on German television. *Top Gear* is broadcast in Germany on the BBC World channel.

Later *Top Gear* aired a spoof ad featuring a Volkswagen Scirocco which Clarkson said went from "Berlin to Warsaw in one tank". It then showed the citizens of Warsaw rushing to board buses and trains as sirens blared, warning of the approaching Germans. One viewer said it was "simply the funniest thing I've ever seen." Polish viewers, though, were not amused.

Clarkson said he feared that it would soon be illegal to make derogatory remarks about people from other countries. He also maintained that it was possible to sum up the people of every nation on Earth with a single word – and the word he chose for Germans was "humourless".

"The other day I spoke to a German car designer for four hours and he failed to make even half an attempt at a joke in all that time," he said. "A Brit can't go four minutes without trying to make someone laugh."

The BBC's Complaints Committee again defended Clarkson, saying that he was merely "using outrageous behaviour to amuse his audience, and that the remarks would not have led to anyone entertaining new or different feelings or concerns about Germans or Germany".

Americans also took flak. One car, Clarkson said took up "less parking space than your average American tourist". Nevertheless *Top Gear* gained a following in the US. In 2003, the *National Review Online* said: "If you wish to get good, informed information from the BBC, the only reasonable place to go is BBC Two's *Top Gear*, just ending its third season on the air. OK, it's a car show, and, true, Americans may not get much from the program's test drives of automobiles known only to readers of *Hemming's Motor News*. But it is the best informational program on the BBC – better than all the science shows; flashier than the prize-less, often clueless quiz programs; shorter than all the historical drivel; smart, funny, well-written, and subversively un-P.C. Recently, when the program was bumped back a bit on the Sunday night line-up without much notice, presenter Jeremy Clarkson tried to regain the BBC's favour by offering to rename the show *The Nelson Mandela Car Show* while series regulars James May and Richard Hammond ostentatiously read copies of the leftwing *Guardian* and flashed their New Age sandals."

But still the critics queued up to shoot him down. The environmentalist Jonathan Porritt called Clarkson an "outstandingly bigoted petrol-head".

"The issue isn't that he just picks on certain groups of people," said Ben Summerskill, chief executive of the gay lobby Stonewall. "It's that he's bullying and revels in causing offence."

Clarkson caused further offence when he responded to the observation that the Duchess of Cornwall was approaching sixty by saying: "That's not as bad as Diana. She was approaching 120 when she entered the tunnel in Paris."

Nevertheless the BBC went to great lengths to defend Clarkson and *Top Gear*, even issuing a statement that read: "We have received a variety of complaints. We acknowledge some viewers do not appreciate the *Top Gear* team's sense of humour but their provocative comments are an integral part of the programme and are not intended to be taken seriously. In addition to making fun of each other, Jeremy Clarkson and his co-presenters frequently make jibes at members of the audience and at individuals and organizations featured in the programme. This is part of the appeal and no one is immune from the team's acerbic comments and observations. We trust most viewers are familiar enough with the style and tone of the show not to take offence."

Despite his detractors Clarkson's TV career continued to blossom. In 2006 he became a guest presenter of *Never Mind the Buzzcocks*. He also sat in as quiz-master on *Have I Got News for You*. He was then voted third hippest celebrity in Britain, after David Tennant and

Fearne Cotton, by the country's eleven and twelve year olds. Then *GQ* named him TV Personality of the Year. Clarkson responded: "It's a great honour to be named the fattest TV presenter in the country." He also made the magazine's list of worst dressed men, albeit behind David Cameron, James May, Pete Doherty, Jonathan Ross and A A Gill.

Chapter Nine – A Disaster Waiting to Happen?

Top Gear was in trouble in September 2006 when co-host Richard Hammond had a near-fatal accident driving a 300-mph jet-car. At Elvington airfield, the car veered off the track and rolled over, before digging itself into the ground upside down. Hammond recovered but the show's safety record faced an enquiry. Clarkson said that Hammond was "a crap driver", but he had only had a few hours training beforehand.

In the *Daily Mail*, motoring correspondent said: "*Top Gear* has long been a disaster that was just waiting to happen… How many viewers, for instance, must wonder if Jeremy Clarkson and the other presenters have acquired an international exemption from speed limits – or if all the police forces of Europe are turning a blind eye – every time we see them racing across the continent in a trio of 200-mph supercars?"

The BBC delayed airing the series until Hammond had made a complete recovery. Filming resumed the following month. The show went on to win the National Television Award for the Most Popular Factual Programme. Accepting the award, Clarkson addressed an aside to Hammond. "I told you if one of us had a car accident we'd win this," he said.

When footage of the crash was broadcast, Clarkson looked straight at the camera and said: "Remember – speed kills." Ofcom received twenty complaints from viewers, citing his tongue-in-cheek manner.

Clarkson pushed the boundaries further, when a two-seater Daihatsu Copen was described as "a bit gay, yes, very ginger beer". This time the BBC did not leap to his defence. The corporation's head of complaints said that there was "no editorial purpose" for the remarks and that Clarkson "supplemented the term 'gay' with a phrase which is rhyming slang for 'queer', there was no doubt it was used in the sense of 'homosexual' and was capable of giving offence."

Initially, Clarkson said that by "ginger beer" he meant that it was "fizzy and a bit like beer. But not like the proper stuff which makes you happy and drunk." If the head of complaints had only called him during his six-month investigation, they could have cleared the whole thing up. Instead, Clarkson simply compounded the offence, saying: "No one's rung me to tell me off. And it wasn't a gay car – it was actually a bit lesbian."

In *Top Gear* magazine, Clarkson had already described the Daihatsu as a "cutie with a folding metal roof, aimed at those with a collection of sunglasses and co-ordinating handbags". Naturally he would not have one in his own garage that then housed a Lamborghini Gallardo Spyder, a Volvo XC90, a Mercedes-Benz SLK55, a Ford Focus and decommissioned military Land Rover. This was not his dream garage. Along with the Lamborghini, he said he would have preferred it housed an Aston Martin V8 Vantage, a

BMW M5, a VW Phaeton, a Rolls-Royce Phantom, a Corvette C6, a Vauxhall Monaro, a Porsche Carrera GT, a Pagani Zonda F, an Alfa Romeo Brera, an Audi RS4 and a Bugatti Veyron. Big garage.

Clarkson then moved to the big screen – or at least his voice did – for the UK version of the Disney-Pixar animated film *Cars*. He played Harv, Lighting McQueen's agent, who was heard over the speaker phone. Perhaps Clarkson was planning a new career in the movies when he cast doubt over the return of *Top Gear*. It seems that, behind the scenes, the presenters wanted to keep the cars as the centre of the show, while the BBC preferred celebrity guests. In March 2007, he wrote in the *Sun*: "After last week's *Top Gear*, the continuity announcer said the show would be back in the summer. Can I just say, here and now, it won't be."

The BBC were adamant that the show would return with a special in the summer and a new series in the autumn. But Clarkson's position seemed unclear and Francie failed to clear up the mystery. Meanwhile Clarkson was stirring things up with the environmentalists – or eco-mentalists as he calls them – again on *Have I Got News for You*. Of the Live Earth benefit concerts opposing climate change, he said: "Rock stars are getting together to solve global warming. Live Earth is committed to being the first carbon-neutral event. Hybrid cars will be used for transport, food will be served in biodegradable containers. And the stage will be illuminated by the light that shines out of Bono's arse."

But Clarkson was not against performing at a benefit himself. He learnt to play the drums. With James May on keyboards and Richard

Hammond on bass guitar, they backed Justin Hawkins, lead singer and guitarist of The Darkness, on the Billy Ocean track "Red Light Spells Danger" for Comic Relief's Red Nose Day. Clarkson related the incompetence of his performance in his *Sunday Times* column. He said that he had always thought the drums were noise that went on in the background of the song. Instead he learnt that the man who keeps time is the single most vital piece of the whole ensemble – and Hammond wanted to kill him.

"The finished product was transmitted on Friday night at ten o'clock," he concluded. "I hope you were all in bed and missed it.

For years Clarkson had taken family holidays on Barbados. In 2007, while there, he met up with Prince Harry. They played tennis, went deep-sea fishing and had dinner together. This gave Clarkson the opportunity to print an exclusive interview with the prince, who complained of the cat-and-mouse game he and his girlfriend, twenty-one-year-old Chelsy Davy, played with the paparazzi.

Jeremy should have taken note. He was snapped on the beach "sporting the biggest potbelly seen since Vanessa Feltz was last pregnant," according to Piers Morgan. "Take some advice from a mate, Jezza," Morgan continued. "Get out of those cars and on to a treadmill before they have to rename your show *Spare Tyres*."

Next Clarkson struck out at Channel Four news presenters, saying all they had to do was turn up for work in a garish tie, read excerpts from the *Guardian* and go home. Jon Snow responded, saying: "Well what do you have to do on a motoring programme? All you have to do is get in the car and push your foot down." Though he did admit watching *Top Gear* on BBC World "in very far-flung places where there's nothing else on telly".

Clarkson then called the Perodua Kelisas the "worst car in the world". It was "unimaginative junk", had a name like a disease and was built in "jungles by people who wear leaves for shoes". He took a sledgehammer to the Kelisa, hung it up on cranes with a one-ton weight attached that putted out it innards, then blew it up with dynamite. The Malaysian parliament raised objections and minister Abdul Raman Suliman said Clarkson was like "a football commentator who couldn't play football". As a repost, this was hardly in the Clarkson league.

More trouble ensued in March 2008 when the *Daily Mirror* revealed Clarkson had been photographed chatting on his mobile phone while driving his Mercedes at 70 mph on a motorway. That May, Clarkson told an audience that he got a speeding ticket for doing 186 mph in a road tunnel. Then in November, the BBC got five hundred complaints after Clarkson joked that lorry drivers spend their time murdering prostitutes.

Next in the firing line was Prime Minister Gordon Brown, who Clarkson called "a one-eye Scottish idiot". Brown had lost sight in one eye as a result of a rugby accident in his teens. Clarkson was forced into making an apology – of sorts.

"I very specifically apologized for making fun of his personal appearance – very specifically," he said. "I have nothing against the Scottish and of course I regret making any remark that might have upset the disabled. But the idiot bit – there is no chance I'll apologize for that."

There was already an online petition to make Jeremy Clarkson prime minister which attracted thousands of signatures. He was already travelling in political circles. David Cameron was a member of the Chipping Norton set. After Cameron became prime minister, Clarkson and Francie were seen with the PM and his wife Samantha at a Christmas party at Rebekah Brooks' house, which was also nearby. Clarkson said the PM's wife smoked his cigarettes, while Cameron and Mrs Brooks talked sausage rolls.

When the phone-hacking scandal broke, but before Brooks was arrested, Clarkson said: "I feel desperately sad Rebekah has resigned, but the cloud does have a silver lining – I can see more of her."

In 2013, he threatened to stand against Ed Miliband in his home town of Doncaster. Miliband had condemned Clarkson in a speech about mental illness. Clarkson, he said, dismissed people who took their own lives as "Johnny Suicides" whose bodies should be left on train tracks rather than delay journeys. To add insult to injury, Miliband lumped Clarkson together with Janet Street-Porter who had said that depression was "'the latest must-have accessory" promoted by the "misery movement".

Plainly Clarkson did not take kindly to being corralled with his arch-enemy when he threatened to take him on politically. He also found he had an ally in London mayor Boris Johnson who commented: "Right idea, Jezza – wrong seat. I hope fervently that the great man can be persuaded to stand against Cleggers in Sheffield, where his majority (unlike Ed's) is very frail indeed."

Clarkson appears constantly amazed that his off-hand remarks put people's backs up. "There are more important things to worry about than what some balding and irrelevant middle-aged man might have said on a crappy BBC Two motoring show," he wrote in his newspaper column.

"I don't believe what I write, any more than you believe what you say," he once quipped to Tony Blair's spin doctor Alastair Campbell.

But why should he worry? By then Clarkson was one of the highest paid presenters on the BBC. While his £1 million salary was eclipsed by Jonathan Ross's £6 million when he was with the corporation and Graham Norton's annual pay, thought to be around £4.5 million, Clarkson was also paid £8.4 million for his stake in a joint venture with BBC Worldwide that exploited *Top Gear*'s global band, along with a £4.86 million dividend payment. He was also in demand on the after-dinner speaking circuit, where he could earn at least £20,000 an evening.

Chapter Ten – The C-Word

In May 2014, Clarkson was called before BBC bosses after the *Daily Mirror* received footage of him trying to pick between two cars using the old rhyme "Eeny, Meany, Miny, Moe…" In two takes he mumbled over the word the *Mirror* took to be "nigger". In the third, which was aired, he replaced it with the word "teacher".

"I've been told by the BBC that if I make one more offensive, remark, anywhere, at any time, I will be sacked," Clarkson said. He insisted he had not used the "n" word that he found "extremely distasteful".

"I use the F-word pretty much constantly and the C-word too, especially when I'm talking about James May. But the N-word? No. It's not in my lexicon," he went on. "It's funny. I've always thought I'd be sacked for something I said. Not for something that actually, I didn't say."

The furore comes just days after *Top Gear* producers had apologized for a "light-hearted" joke by Clarkson in Myanmar and Thailand in which he referred to a "slope" on a bridge as an Asian man crossed a makeshift structure built by the presenters. Producer Andy Wilman said they were unaware it was a racially offensive term for Asians used in countries such as Australia and the United States and regretted any offence caused. All this added more fuel to the "I Hate Jeremy Clarkson" page on Facebook and comedian Jon

Holmes then apologized to Radio Four listeners for using the C-word – Clarkson.

Would that be the end of it?

"I seriously doubt it," said Clarkson. "Even the angel Gabriel would struggle with that hanging over his head. It's inevitable that one day, someone, somewhere will say that I've offended them, and that will be that."

Meanwhile, Clarkson's personal life had also been taking a battering. In 2011, the *Daily Mirror* revealed that he had a secret mistress, forty-two-year-old blonde Phillipa "Pippa" Sage. The newspaper alleged that they had shared a suite in a hotel in Oslo when *Top Gear Live* was on tour there. Later they had been seen together in Australia and South Africa. After Clarkson returned home to Francie and the family, Phillipa denied having an affair. "Jeremy and I are friends," she told the newspaper. "I have worked with him, er them, for years."

When told she had been seen entering Clarkson's hotel suite in the early hours, she said: "What? I often stay in colleagues' hotel rooms – that's not unusual."

Clarkson, who was on holiday with Francie in Barbados at the time, also denied the affair. "I'm surprised to find that I'm the new Tiger Woods," he said.

The *Mirror* then unearthed a cutting from his motoring column the previous year, headlined: "Lie back, leggy Phillipa, while I have some fun". In it, Clarkson raved about the Maserati Quattroporte – and the blonde in the back, who he introduced as "our green-room director Phillipa, who's so tall she's actually measured in hands". His nickname for her was "Little Horse" because of her height of six-foot. She had been a beautician and masseuse before she joined *Top Gear*.

The papers reported that fifty-one-year-old Clarkson was having a mid-life crisis. A month later Clarkson moved into a flat in Bayswater. "When I moved recently into an unfurnished flat I spent the first evening sitting on the floor, wondering what is essential and what really, is not," he said. "I'd need a fridge and a cooker. I'd take my clothes to the launderette – and I'd need some pornography as well so that would mean I'd need the internet."

He was no more domesticated than the last time he had lived alone. "To cheer myself up, I tried to make a cup of coffee," he said, "but the machine I'd bought to do this decided that what I'd like instead is no coffee at all... So if you do lose your job and you end up living in a barn, with just a fire to keep you warm and nothing to eat but what you can find in a hedge, be happy. Because you'll be having a much better life than me."

He claimed that he needed the west London flat to be near the BBC's studios. The weekends, though, would be spent back in the Cotswolds. Clarkson protested that he and Francie were still together and they always had a flat in London, but when she came to town she stayed in a penthouse, while he was seen struggling unshaven with the self-service check-out in Sainsbury's.

Then Phillipa was dropped from the show. "Jeremy could only continue on the tour if Phillipa wasn't involved," the *Mirror* was told.

Later that year, Clarkson admitted having got a gagging order on his first wife, then lifted the injunction that prevent her speaking about her alleged seven-year affair with him after he had married Francie. Alex then took the opportunity to go on television to say as much. "I still love Jeremy," she said. "He got the injunction because he had something to hide. I can prove we had an affair. The truth will out. We did have an affair for seven years."

On his next trip to Australia, Clarkson was photographed lounging on a £1.3-million speedboat surrounded by attractive young women. The *Sunday Mirror*'s headline was: "Missing home Jeremy?"

The following year, Clarkson and Phillipa were seen holidaying together in Rome. His daughter Emily, now eighteen, posted on her Twitter account: "#ThingsMyDaddyTaughtMe Don't get caught."

Phillipa continued to claim they were "just good friends". Nevertheless there was still speculation that the Clarksons' marriage was on the rocks.

In March 2013, Clarkson blew up at photographers in Australia when they snapped him with Phillipa. He screamed: "You can take them out of England, but you just can't take the convict out of them!"

That August the paparazzi caught them again, this time kissing in the beach-side taverna on a Greek island. The bikini-clad Phillipa was running her fingers through his hair during a booze-fuelled lunch. The *Daily Mirror* headline told them to "Get a vroom".

The following May, they were seen together again drinking outside a pub in the Cotswold village of Kingham, just six miles from his home in Chipping Norton which "he shares at weekends with his long-suffering wife Frances and their three children". The *Express on Sunday* praised Francie for sticking by him despite the affair, which it had been said was broken off the previous year. Of the blonde masseuse, the paper said: "Her soothing fingers will undoubtedly be a blessing to Jeremy in these tricky times."

This was happening just at the time Clarkson was being pilloried in the press for his "eeny, meany, miny, mo" remarks. Meanwhile, Francie was on holiday in Mallorca, it was said, "celebrating the end of their twenty-one-year marriage". Alex was back in the press saying that Francie "deserves every penny she gets" from any divorce settlement: "It is her hard work that has made him into the idol he is today."

She was sympathetic to Francie and wished the couple "a happy, healthy, sensible divorce". And she added: "I don't think he ever loved his wife – he loved me."

Alex now claimed to have fallen out of love with Clarkson. She also said she believed that he has found true love with Phillipa Sage.

"When I first saw the pictures in the paper, I knew that he had fallen in love with her," she said. "I think he will be very happy with her. I think he's a serial monogamist, I don't think he's a fly-by-night philanderer."

Soon after Jeremy and Phillipa were seen house-hunting in Warwickshire. The *Express on Sunday* commented: "Patient Pippa already seems to spend a great deal of time cleaning his spark plugs and checking his exhaust; although she may be relieved that he doesn't need servicing quite as often as he used to."

But, as always, Clarkson was not much bothered what anyone thought and no one doubts his ability to bounce back both personally and professionally. However, he could console himself that Piers Morgan has lost his job on CNN, telling his nemesis: "You can always get a job as my punchbag."

Clarkson, of course, can take any punch the press or the pundits throw at him. The rest of us await, with bated breath, his next misdemeanour which is guaranteed to infuriate and amuse in equal measure. Meanwhile we will go on watching his television programmes, reading his newspaper columns, turning up at his live shows and buying his books and DVDs in every increasing numbers.

Epilogue

Clarkson was in Russia on a Top Gear tour during the Eeny, Meeny, Miny, Mo brouhaha. It was then that he heard his mother Shirley had died. He wrote movingly about his loss in his column in the *Sunday Times*.

"I knew that if I wept, which is what I wanted to do because I was very close to my mother," he said, "the *Daily Mirror* would run pictures and claim they were tears of shame. It was a gruesome time."

Returning to England Clarkson had to cede the Paddington Bear Shirley had made for Christmas in 1971 to his sister because "she's a lawyer". However, he got to keep the cereal bowl with rabbits on he had as a child and a mildly fire damaged Dralon chair his father had bought for £4 in 1972. His mother, being a practical sort, had put her affairs in order and thrown the rest of her stuff in a skip.

Then the news broke that Clarkson and Piers Morgan had ended their long-running feud. They posted a selfie on Twitter showing the two of them red-faced and grinning with their arms around each other's shoulders. Morgan admitted that alcohol had been consumed.

So are we seeing a new, softer Clarkson? I doubt it. And would we really want one?

10018851R00051

Printed in Great Britain
by Amazon.co.uk, Ltd.,
Marston Gate.